Summary

Of

The Man Who Broke Capitalism

How Jack Welch Gutted the Heartland and Crushed the Soul of Corporate America—and How to Undo His Legacy

By

David Gelles

Danielle Patterson

Table of Contents

Introduction

In America, we love our managers more than our chiefs. She says the general population has more confidence in Presidents than it does in government officials or clerics. In any event, when our legends end up being law breakers, we can't resist the urge to need a greater amount of them. Jack Welch was Chief of General Electric from 1981 to 2001, twenty years that formed the world we possess today. Welch comprehended the force of the financial exchange and utilized it to compensate investors.

He was a philosophical progressive who zeroed in on amplifying benefits to the detriment of all else. During the 1970s, a framework of financial specialists rethought the motivation behind the company and its job in the public eye. Jack Welch chose to steer GE in a sharp new heading. He embraced systems proclaimed by the financial progressives on the right and formulated his own hired fighter turns. He terminated specialists in large numbers, persuaded that a more modest head include was a beneficial end by its own doing.

Welch supported offshoring and sent a huge number of association occupations abroad to nations like Mexico. GE made almost 1,000 acquisitions during Welch's residency, going through some $130 billion purchasing up organizations. GE sold approximately 408 organizations for about $10.6 billion. No organization had at any point done such countless arrangements so rapidly. Frequently, the arrangements were debacles; they frequently took GE a long way from its modern roots.

GE's money division turned into GE's focal point of gravity, representing 40% of incomes and 60 percent of benefits. Income targets were accomplished utilizing questionable bookkeeping strategies. Black box monetary models and restricted public revelations managed the cost of minimal comprehension of GE's internal functions. Welch utilized them to remunerate investors with a gusher of buybacks and profits. Welch's rule as President of General Electric spread over thirty years and four U.S. presidents.

Business colleges treated Welch like a prophet, transforming his methodologies into contextual investigations and educational programs. Welch was the representation of American, dominant man private enterprise with the crown jewels to demonstrate it. Welch made General Electric the most significant organization on the planet. However, his momentary dynamic prompted a winding of decline. GE required a $139 billion salvage from the Obama organization and a venture from Warren Buffett to fight off breakdown.

In 2021, leaders reported an arrangement to separate GE. Welch's inheritance was discolored by the breakdown of GE, yet his thoughts are as yet persuasive. Welchism credits moral worth to material achievement, giving mogul Chiefs a facade of ethicalness. Welchist perspective takes on a Darwinian mentality toward the work market. GE was a trailblazer in a hierarchical plan and chief preparation.

Welch contaminated another age of business pioneers with his qualities. Today, there are half as many blue-collar positions in the US as there were in 1980. GE's Welch introduced a period of control leader remuneration. President pay grew 940% starting around 1978. During a similar time, the typical specialist's compensation has expanded by 12%.

Cutting position, wild deal-making, reevaluating, and financialization became far and wide under Welch. The present Presidents make 368 fold the amount of laborers did in 1980. Welch had the option to look as GE went to pieces and deplored the wrongdoings of other corporate agitators. In retirement, he changed himself into an administration master offering motivation to another age. The present Chiefs are starting to communicate a recharged obligation to serve all partners, including laborers and the climate. Getting rid of Welchism will be an imposing test, yet there are provisional indications of progress.

Chapter One

The Most Valuable Company in the World

"I plan to blow up the Queen Mary"

John Francis Welch Jr. was named CEO of General Electric a month after Ronald Reagan was chosen president. GE's result represented a full rate point of total national output, its CEO instructed an unwavering labor force of 400,000 people. Its TVs, fridges, and toaster ovens were in endless American homes. GE was viewed as a trailblazer in administration reasoning, setting the norm by which armies of executives are prepared. GE's past CEOs had advised presidents and reshaped business college educational programs.

The determination interaction required years and had all the showy behaviors of cardinals picking another pope. Welch succeeded Reginald Jones, who had run General Electric for 10 years. Jones was viewed as the most impressive President in America. GE didn't develop dangerously fast during his residency, however, it safeguarded its remaining as a model corporate resident. Welch was fretful, hasty, and uncouth.

Welch wore pants and rolled-up shirtsleeves at whatever point he could pull off it. GE had "supplanted a legend with a live wire," the Money Road Diary joked upon Welch's appearance. Welch visited GE joint endeavor in Japan where ultrasound machines were being made. "The cycle resembled nothing I had found in the US," Welch said. NBC's 1980 narrative, on the off chance that Japan Can, For what reason Can't We?

GE's Jack Welch was a fanatic in all he did. At the point when he dominated, a big part of GE's income came from organizations tracing all the way back to the Edison time. Rather than attempting to fix U.S. production, Welch deserted it and would before long begin delivery occupations abroad. GE's stock cost hadn't moved in years. Welch needed reliable, better-than-expected income development through the financial cycle.

Welch accepted GE would have been the most important organization on the planet. He had no clue exactly the way that widely inclusive the change would be.

"Generous Electric"

General Electric acquainted the world with power plants and glowing lights. Thomas Edison himself flipped the switch at the principal American power station in 1882. GE's researchers helped win the universal conflicts and won Nobel Prizes, as well. The organization assumed a fundamental part in the American work to win The Second Great War. GE was among the principal American organizations to offer its representatives retirement designs, a portion of benefits, medical coverage, and extra security.

The organization fabricated one of the main genuine corporate grounds, on a 92 section of land site outside Cleveland.

GE grasped the benefit of taking astounding consideration of its laborers. GE utilized its immense assets to take excellent consideration of its workers. It offered a benefit-sharing arrangement, medical advantages, higher wages, and more to lift the general mood and move laborers. GE was so unselfish in these years that it procured the moniker "Liberal Electric". The total dispensed for financial backers was an unassuming 3.9 percent of deals.

GE considered itself to be a piece of an interconnected entire, where workers and society didn't assume a lower priority in relation to investors. In 1960, General Electric's motto was "Progress Is Our Most Significant Item". Under Welch, the organization put 10% of its benefits into innovative work. The New Arrangement revived the economy with huge interest in the foundation, making a great many positions. Brilliant Time of Free enterprise was a stretch when large numbers of incomparable American managers were at their best.

Robert Wood Johnson, the director of Johnson and Johnson, made the organization's "Philosophy" in 1943. The Philosophy is a relic of the Brilliant Age, protecting in golden the unmistakable needs of that age's most persuasive finance managers. It swore that leaders would be "people of ability, schooling, experience, and capacity". From 1948 to 1979, specialist pay developed couple with laborer efficiency. GE turned into a model manager, the sort of organization where a sketchy youngster could make a profession.

It was a righteous cycle that transformed America into the world's most noteworthy monetary motor. The working class developed, shopper burning through swelled, and new organizations were established.

"With my nose pressed up against the glass"

Welch was short, irascible, and had a stammer. He diverted these detriments into a fretful, contentious character. Welch's desire in life was "to make 1,000,000," he wrote in his yearbook. His serious nature fit him well for an undeniably aggressive economy. Welch concentrated on synthetic design, and acquired Ph.D. in compound designing.

In 1960, he joined the GE plastics plant in Massachusetts; beginning compensation was $10,500 per year. A year into his residency, Welch's supervisor let him know he was getting a $1,000 raise. Welch was eager and stretched his GE group to the edges. He exploded a plant while pushing his group to develop, and pulled off it. "At the point when individuals commit errors, the last thing they need is discipline," he said.

In 1968, he was elevated to the top of the organization's plastic business. Welch accepted cutbacks would assist him with standing apart from different competitors for the Chief work. GE's Apparatus Park was the origination of millions of GE toaster ovens, clothes washers, and coolers. 23,000 individuals worked there before Welch came on the scene. In 1951, GE was at the level of its after-war aspirations, this complex was its machines division's base camp.

GE Credit Corp., the organization's money division, would later become GE Capital. His administration style denoted an extreme change for an organization like GE that would in general be stodgy and formal. Jack Welch was the direct opposite of what you would anticipate that GE Chief Reg Jones should pick. He was merciless in his cuts and burning in his studies of underperformers. "Everyone was stunned when Jack landed the position," says Ken Langone, a long-term GE board part.

"The most competitive enterprise on earth"

GE's new Chief spread out his vision for the organization in a discourse in 1987. He believed GE should turn into a monetary force to be reckoned with, in addition to a light maker. GE workers would need to "see things as they are" and face hard insights, Welch said. GE was to turn into "the train pulling the GNP, not the rear following it". Welch's discourse was a harbinger of what might turn into his all-consuming desire.

He needed to make GE the most serious endeavor around, the most important organization on the planet. The discourse was a lemon. Welch took advantage of significant changes in the climate. The scholarly upheaval had been flowing through intellectual, financial, lawful, and political circles. Government assistance, and social well-being nets would definitely prompt unremarkableness and lack of concern, they accepted.

Friedrich A. Friedman took Hayek's hypothesis of benefits thought process and applied it to enterprises. He contended that the social obligation of business is to expand its benefits. It was an industrialist cri de coeur, begging chiefs to embrace the benefits thought process. In 1969, High Court Equity Powell cautioned business pioneers that their lifestyle was in danger. The following year he composed a reminder illustrating a strategy to safeguard financial matters.

In the years that followed, large businesses spent tons of cash on governmental issues at remarkable rates. Friedman contended that organizations exist exclusively to improve their investors. In 1976, two teachers developed the Friedman regulation in their paper "Hypothesis of the Firm" Jensen and Meckling contended that Chiefs ought to be lavishly compensated with stock to adjust their motivating forces to their organization's monetary exhibition. Reagan stacked his organization with corporate supporters. Unrestricted economy creed had arisen as predominant scholarly power molding legislative issues and economies in the West.

Jack Welch was the primary Chief to embrace the plan of investor power really. He outfits the entirety of GE to make it genuine and introduce a new, merciless period of American private enterprise. In his self-portrayal, Welch basically parroted Milton Friedman's perspective on business.

Chapter Two

Neutron Jack

The "Campaign Against Loyalty"

Welch's managerial style was characterized by a high level of screaming and a lack of empathy. He was a harsh critic of managers who appeared to know less about their own company than he did. In Welch's first year as CEO, GE laid off 35,000 people or about 9% of the workforce. The moniker "Neutron Jack" was given to Jack Welch because of his managerial approach. Except for nine other Fortune 500 businesses, GE was the most lucrative. Welch arrived at GE with the zealous belief that the company employed much too many employees.

Welch was irritated by the notion that employees turned on GE for security and stability. Employees should not demand too much from the organization, he urged. Welch debunked the concept that mass layoffs were a last-resort option employed exclusively in emergencies. The lowest-performing 10% of GE employees should be laid go every year. It was a callous decree that ensured that tens of thousands of people would be laid off, regardless of how well GE performed.

GE CEO Jack Welch wanted his employees to feel they were doing their best for the company. He made continuous downsizing seem essential, even normal, by whitewashing enormous layoffs. Welch framed the devastation of livelihoods as an act of God, absolving himself of personal responsibility. Welch's whole twenty-year rule was marked by relentless staff elimination. While Welch was CEO of GE, hundreds of thousands of workers lost their employment.

Welch cut his company's numbers in the 1980s by firing food service workers, security guards, and janitors. Welch moved to offshore when outsourcing failed to meet his objectives. He came close to achieving the same goal by relocating huge manufacturing activities from cities like Fort Wayne, Indiana, to Mexico and Brazil. Despite GE's lengthy and occasionally tumultuous relationship with labor, Welch was able to accomplish all of this. GE's headcount in the United States plummeted throughout the 1980s and early 1990s.

The company added 20,000 jobs in other countries and extensively invested in its business in India. As GE moved production offshore, the geographical distribution of those employment shifted drastically. General Electric's continual reduction drained the company's morale. Welch's leadership style was rife with toxic masculine traits. He made fun of the weak, wanted complete devotion, and was never content.

His methods had drained the enthusiasm from what had once been a great firm. He was awarded the "Toughest Boss in America" by Fortune magazine. Welch's preferred method of describing terminating someone was to remark that they should be "shot." When considering layoffs, he used a lot of threatening language. As unions weakened, workers in the United States received a less and smaller share of the economic pie. Wage growth has slowed, and blue-collar employees have had their gains reversed.

"The Pac-Man model"

Following the reduction, Jack Welch looked for new methods to grow General Electric. He acquired RCA for $6.3 billion in 1985, making it the biggest non-oil acquisition ever. With the help of the Reagan government, GE was able to take up RCA. GE's yearly revenues increased from $28 billion to more than $40 billion. With RCA on board, Welch predicted that GE would become "one dynamite corporation."

Welch cut RCA's headcount from roughly 88,000 to 36,000 in a couple of months. GE's medical systems division was weaker than the company had anticipated. Orders dried up rapidly, and profits vanished. But, according to Wall Street's bizarre reasoning, it didn't really matter. GE's television set business has grown to become one of the world's largest.

GE chose Roger Ailes to oversee CNBC, the business news channel, in 1993. Roger Ailes was named to lead NBC's political reporting division by Welch. Welch is said to have snuck into the NBC newsroom and persuaded executives to call George W. Bush's election in 2000. GE Capital was already active in the buyout sector, having provided financing for some of the most significant transactions of the time. Only eight months after it closed, Kidder became the epicenter of the financial industry's greatest crisis.

After Kidder Peabody, the investment bank was discovered to be fabricating earnings, GE was slapped with a $1.2 billion loss. In 1987, GE had to lay off 1,000 individuals, or 20% of its workforce, and Kidder's New York headquarters had to close. The purchases of RCA and Kidder Peabody by GE demonstrated that expansion could be achieved through acquisition rather than construction. As GE's foray into finance progressed, investors began to notice what he was up to. Since Welch's entrance, the company's stock had increased by 250 percent by 1987.

Welch reorganized the economy in ways that went far beyond GE. By the conclusion of the decade, 143 of the Fortune 500 companies (or 28 percent) had been bought. Companies were being purchased with borrowed funds and loaded with debt by buyout firms.

"Eating your own mother"

Welch started actively expanding into the insurance sector in 1983. He paid $90 million for American Mortgage Insurance and $1.1 billion for Employers Reinsurance Corporation. GE Capital had $370 billion in assets and activities in over fifty countries when he resigned. By chasing money wherever it might be found, GE Capital flourished. GE Capital had less than 7,000 workers and $67 million in profits in 1977.

The division had grown to almost 89,000 employees by the time Jack Welch resigned in 1999. GE's finance division formerly accounted for more than half of the company's income. He leveraged it to lock in low loan rates, reduce GE's taxes, and smooth out quarterly results. GE was able to borrow money at a cheaper rate than its competitors due to its AAA credit rating. As GE became increasingly sophisticated, each quarter delivered the exact figure that Wall Street demanded.

Unrelated events were synchronized in such a way that the balance sheet was miraculously smoothed out. It was a never-ending cycle of speculation that ensured GE's earnings grew at a steady, predictable pace. GE made a $1.54 billion profit and received $600 million in tax benefits as a result of a complicated transaction with Lockheed Martin. To cover the expense of decommissioning those factories, GE developed a plan to take a massive $2.3 billion write-off. Over 1,000 individuals have lost their employment.

Many purchases were made by GE officials racing to meet Welch's lofty earnings projections. "When we execute an acquisition, of course, we're purchasing earnings," says GE Capital's CFO. Gary Wendt, the former CEO of GE Capital, dismisses the importance of mergers and acquisitions. The finance section of GE was instrumental in lowering the company's tax burden. In 1997, GE and other corporations secured a legal reform that allowed them to avoid paying the IRS billions of dollars.

Welch purposefully obscured the inner workings of the company's profit machine. GE made financial data difficult to obtain, but Welch knew how to sell a tale. He began diverting some of GE's top staff to the investor relations department in the late 1980s. He ushered in a new era of corporate self-promotion without restraint. Buybacks essentially allow firms to control the price of their own shares.

Companies were prohibited from manipulating their own stock price under the Securities Act of 1933. Welch took advantage of the situation and launched the world's largest stock repurchase program at the time. Many business giants of the time were baffled by the use of so many resources for buybacks rather than research and development or worker pay. Major firms were spending approximately 30% of their profits on buybacks by the late 1980s. In the 1990s, this percentage climbed to almost 50%.

Today's average American worker would earn around $102,000 per year, roughly double what he or she does now. Despite these alarming figures, buybacks are nevertheless popular in the business world. Few firms have spent more money over the years repurchasing their own stock. During Welch's tenure, financial services became the fastest-growing sector of the US economy. Thousands of bankers and attorneys were employed as a result of the proliferation of banks and trading businesses, as well as mergers and acquisitions.

Financial services began to account for a growing and increasing share of America's gross domestic product. In 1993, Jack Welch's GE surpassed Exxon Mobil as the world's most valuable firm. GE was able to make more money with fewer employees thanks to financialization. By the conclusion of Welch's tenure, GE had grown to a value of $600 billion.

Chapter Three

That's Why They Got Hired

"Jobs may come and go"

IBM promoted a "cradle to grave" culture in which employees have almost assured a job for the rest of their lives. Customer service, quality, and individual respect are three basic organizational values developed by Thomas J. Watson. Layoffs were unheard of, and IBM retooled its marketing efforts in 1985 to separate itself from GE. At the time, IBM's 60,000 layoffs were the greatest mass layoff in history. Welch considered labor to be an expense rather than an advantage.

In the 1980s alone, the top 500 corporations in the United States cut their workforce by three million employees. By letting go of staff, he was able to produce $6.3 billion in value. For $9.4 billion, he sold Scott Paper to Kimberly-Clark. In 1996, he returned to the strategies that had won him such a large sum of money. Jacques Nasser was an outspoken supporter of Jack Welch.

He attempted to replicate GE's personnel classification system of A, B, and C players. Nasser's attempts to diversify into junkyards, repair shops, and other businesses alarmed Ford employees. The downsizing that GE's Jack Welch ushered through changed the wealth distribution across the country. Now, corporate profits are

23

soaring, and CEO pay is skyrocketing, while the wealth of ordinary employees has scarcely increased. Welchism was a virus that had been incubating inside GE for some time and was now spreading.

"I want a revolution"

A case study from Harvard Business School: "A barometer of American management methods," according to General Electric. Charles Coffin was hailed as the "Father of Professional Management" when he took over GE in 1892. To support an ever-more complex company, GE spent extensively on management training programs. "GE mints business executives the way West Point mints generals," as Management Today, a publication for org-chart fans, put it. He wanted to see and be seen by the company's top executives. Crotonville was a private executive business school.

The center was the first of its sort, inspiring IBM, Hitachi, and Boeing to build similar facilities. This was a capitalist boot camp, designed to select out those who lacked the tenacity necessary for the grueling duties ahead. Welchism 101 was a crash education in bare-knuckle profit-maximizing and expense minimization.

"No bozos,"

GE executives were seen to be the pinnacle of corporate America. Welch cultivated a legion of acolytes who absorbed his methods.

Companies including 3M, Amgen, Arctic Cat, Boeing, Chrysler, Fiat, Goodyear, Great Lakes Chemical, SPX, and Stanley were run by them. "GE became the source," Bill George argues, "and they diffused GE thought across American business." Larry Bossidy was the chairman and CEO of AlliedSignal, a struggling corporation.

His shareholder letters were nearly identical to Jack Welch's annual missives for GE. Bossidy wanted to be his own boss after a decade under Welch's shadow. He curtailed capital investment, laid off 6,200 people, and took a hard line with suppliers." Then it became fashionable under Jack Welch." Larry "the Knife". The doomed merger would have given GE fresh exposure to valuable industrial divisions and increased its market share in important regions.

After a year of arduous discussions, GE walked away, thwarting Welch's final coup attempt. Bossidy terminated 15,800 employees, or 13% of Honeywell's workforce, in the first year after the merger was canceled. John Trani, who had climbed through the ranks of GE Medical Systems, departed to join Stanley Works as CEO. Frederick T. Stanley created Stanley in 1843 with the goal of creating a corporation with "unsurpassed customer service, product innovation, and integrity." Stanley's annual shareholder meeting in

1999 was held in Columbus, Ohio, rather than in Connecticut, where the business was located.

Like Bossidy, GE's Jack Trani got the title "Neutron Jack" for himself. Employees were furious, revenues were flatlining, and the stock was in freefall. "Where is your American pride?" another employee questioned Trani. GE Executive at Stanley: I'm happy to be a citizen of the United States of America. We just have different perspectives on the world. According to calculations, the company's strategy would have saved the US government roughly $30 million each year in taxes.

"They have turned their backs on the United States of America," says a congressman. One of Welch's senior subordinates, Paolo Fresco, departed GE to become chairman of Fiat SpA. Paolo wished to bring Welchism to Italy, where many of the characteristics of America's Golden Age of Capitalism remained. Paolo paid $350 million for a Michigan tool firm and $4.3 billion on a Wisconsin heavy equipment manufacturer in 1998. He also pushed to increase the company's finance activities while simultaneously reducing workers. "He's the finest CEO in the United States," Fresco said.

Stanley was still suffering from Trani's mismanagement five years later. What worked at GE, however, didn't work as well at Fiat. Fiat's stock had plummeted 65 percent by 2003, and Fresco had stepped down. At Goodyear, Stanley Gault increased revenue and established a collaborative, inventive culture. Tomas Tiller built an American business while maintaining the majority of its production in the United States.

According to Bill George, who attracted Omar Ishrak to Medtronic, another Welch follower departed GE after believing he didn't have the backing he needed to innovate and develop new technologies. "Jack didn't have a love affair with the individual hourly employee at GE," Tiller explains. That means paying a reasonable salary to his staff while keeping his own income in control for Tiller.

"If it's not Boeing, I'm not going"

Aside from GE, there is one other corporation that has faced the brunt of Welchism's effects: Boeing. Boeing was created in 1916 by William Boeing, and planes like the 707, 737, and 747 helped introduce commercial passenger jets to the masses. Boeing paid $13.3 billion for McDonnell Douglas in 1997. The merger was a sort of victory lap for Boeing, allowing it to gobble up its last significant domestic competitor, but it would change the firm in ways that GE could not have predicted. He started at GE the same year as Welch and rose through the ranks of the company's aviation engines business.

"McDonnell Douglas acquired Boeing with Boeing's money," said Woodrow Wilson. It was a dead ringer for his mentor, and it drained morale among Boeing's tight-knit ranks. Boeing said in 1998 that it will cut 53,000 employees and embrace outsourcing, a year after generously acquiring McDonnell Douglas. He channeled Welch's blunt honesty when they pushed back. Then, in 2001, Boeing took a choice that shocked the business world.

Boeing stated that the objective was to build "a new, smaller corporate core focused on shareholder value." The relocation was sparked by GE, which had its headquarters in Fairfield, Pennsylvania. Kyle Smith describes the McDonnell Douglas Company as "a bunch of corporate ninjas." After getting caught up in a government procurement scam, GE executive Jim Condit was forced to retire. Boeing was hurting on the inside, despite the stock price rising. "If there is a reverse takeover, with the McDonnell mindset pervading Boeing, then Boeing is destined to mediocrity," Jim Collins, a management professor, remarked in 2000. With Condit gone, Stonecipher was named CEO, and Boeing was now led by a man who had learned from Welch himself.

"Manager of the Century"

As the twentieth century came to a conclusion, Jack Welch was riding high with GE, the world's most valuable firm. Approximately 8,000 English language pieces on Welch appeared annually during his final years at GE, most of them adoring in tone. In 1999, while Donald Trump was considering a presidential run, he dubbed Jack Welch "perhaps the greatest corporate leader in the history of a big corporation." He's a fantastic individual. It was not unusual to see headlines like "How to Win."

On Forbes' list of the 400 wealthiest Americans, he is ranked 376th. Welch was able to play a couple of rounds at Augusta National Golf Club at GE's annual conference, which was held near the Masters' home course. When Welch retired, his total salary package was worth $122.5 million. Welch presided over a string of explosive controversies at General Electric during his two decades as CEO. Defrauding the government, setting the price of specific items, and embezzling foreign aid were all discovered by GE brass.

Under Welch, the company's reputation as a decent corporate citizen weakened as well. The Business Roundtable, an important club of CEOs founded by Welch two decades before, updated its mission statement in 1997 to accord with Friedman's theory. The Business Roundtable, an important club of CEOs founded by GE two decades before, updated its mission statement that year. Summers stated, "Any honest Democrat will recognize that we are now all Friedmanites." Jack Welch, the CEO of General Electric, redefined what it meant to be a great American enterprise.

More big companies followed GE's lead and began outsourcing and offshoring. 848,000 industrial jobs were lost in the United States during the 1990s. The divide between output and remuneration had grown to a chasm by the time Welch resigned. And Felix Rohatyn, the investment banker who organized Welch's RCA purchase, had already seen through the ruse. Arthur Levitt, the chairman of the Securities and Exchange Commission (SEC), cautioned in 1998 that firms were using quarterly results as "a numbers game."

"Too many business executives, auditors, and analysts are engaged in a game of nods and winks," he remarked. Although GE wasn't specifically mentioned, it was clear who Levitt was referring to. However, the warning voices were in the minority, and Welch emerged victorious. He chastised overly complicated organizations and said that mass layoffs were a moral obligation. He continued, "Hate bureaucracy, and don't be scared to use the term 'hate.'" Welch also pushed staff to be harsh in their evaluations of one another and to weed out the weak.

Chapter Four

The GE Glow

"The perfect selection"

The question of who would follow Welch as CEO hung big over GE and the business community at large during Welch's last years as CEO. He joined GE in 1982 and rose through the ranks to become the president of the company's transportation business, which produced locomotives. Nardelli adopted a harsh approach with suppliers in the early 1990s. Welch's downsizing had decimated GE's power turbines division, which was now led by John Nardelli. "We will be 'wide paint-brushed' as a bunch of fools again," he said in a meeting with workers.

Welch had wrung a profit out of $9.7 billion in sales by the time he was ready to leave. The next of the three leading contenders, Jim McNerney, was in charge of GE's lighting sector. He was assigned command of GE's aviation engines group, which included a scheme to offer companies and billionaires customized versions of Boeing's 737. Only eleven planes had been sold after four years. Welch could even fly in luxury because GE would take the first order.

Jeff Immelt joined GE after receiving his MBA from Harvard Business School. His father had worked in the aircraft industry at

GE. In 1994, he was named head of the plastics division's Americas region. He, on the other hand, struggled to meet Welch's lofty profit objectives. Immelt, at 6 feet 4 inches tall, towered above Welch.

Under Welch, Immelt didn't take long to embrace the black arts of creative accounting. GE's plastic facilities in Asia didn't create their own basic components; instead, they got them from plants in the United States and Europe. These transfers of commodities from one GE plastics unit to another were reported as sales according to GE's accounting systems. When his figures didn't match up, Immelt found a method to leverage this to his advantage. "They all exceeded every expectation we set for them," Welch says of Welch, Nardelli, McNerney, and Immelt. Welch drew Ken Langone, the GE director, aside at a party at Crotonville the week before Immelt took over and gave him a word of warning.

"Very bright people"

Other senior GE executives started hunting for new employment as the contest dwindled down to Nardelli, McNerney, and Immelt. "When I was at GE, that viewpoint came in helpful."

Larry Johnston, one of the long-shot prospects to follow Welch, departed GE in April 2001 to lead the supermarket chain Albertsons. Before the business disclosed bad quarterly results, one GE executive sold shares for a profit of $25 million. Bennett's techniques that he learned from Welch failed him at both organizations. Executives at GE were offered multimillion-dollar contracts that guaranteed them a comfortable retirement. There was a fanatical adherence to reaching quarterly results, with little attention on long-term planning.

"If it hit them in the head, they wouldn't know strategy," says one former Rotman School dean. Welchism, on the other hand, had to pay a price.

"Prove Jack wrong,"

Home Depot's credit card program was administered by GE Capital, and Langone, the originator of Home Depot, served on the GE board of directors. Welch's autocratic manner was exemplified by his inability to see his three protégés functioning together once he was gone. Nardelli was furious when he found out he had lost out to Immelt. He eliminated middle management, consolidated decision-making, and lowered costs. To enforce some discipline, he brought in more muscle from GE.

"I have no idea what happened to Bob," says Jim Langone, co-founder of Home Depot. Langone and the rest of the Home Depot board of directors had agreed to pay him a salary that would have made Welch blush. But, as someone who grew up in GE's command and control system, the company's occasionally chaotic ethos was anathema to Nardelli. To close watchers of the business world, it looked like Nardelli was on a mission to prove to Welch that his choice of Immelt was a mistake. "One of Bob's concerns, as I look back, was that he never got over the fact that he didn't receive the GE position," says Home Depot co-founder Bob Langone.

When Jack Welch left GE, the company's relationship with Home Depot swiftly deteriorated. Home Depot's stock fell 8% during his tenure, while Lowe's stock climbed 180 percent. Several Cerberus officials had worked with him at GE, and despite the fact that Nardelli had no expertise in the car sector, just as he had no experience in retail, he was allowed free reign and quickly put his Welchian techniques to work. When the financial crisis struck, automakers looked to Washington for assistance, but the exorbitant interest rates on those loans simply accelerated the inevitable. Welch's subordinates have presided over two of the ten greatest corporate failures in American history.

Nardelli defended himself and his firm in front of the Senate, which was looking into the bailout, as one of his final actions on the job. After leaving GE, McNerney, the other loser in the contest to follow Welch, appeared to have greater success. Immelt, who was appointed in late 2000 as CEO of 3M, a Minnesota-based international company that creates chemicals, Scotch tape, Post-it Notes, and other products, was gone within 10 days after taking the post. He used Six Sigma to try to codify what had been a somewhat haphazard, creative culture. The enhanced rigor went well beyond the evaluation of new items.

Simultaneously, he embarked on a cost-cutting spree, reducing budgets across the board. He proceeded to bring the Welch playbook to 3M after that. McNerney looked to have re-energized 3M to outsiders. 3M agreed to a meager $12 million settlement without admitting any wrongdoing. 3M returned to its old, quirky ways after McNerney's departure.

"By its very nature, the invention is a disordered process," the new CEO explained. The former chief of GE's aviation engines division was on his way to Boeing.

"We had no idea"

He inherited a corporation that had branched out into practically every field imaginable. GE was as vulnerable to a black swan event like 9/11 as any other corporation in the US economy. "This is a rough day," Immelt told an investor over the phone. Welch has gone into practically every area imaginable in his ambition to make GE the most valuable corporation on the planet. "It's impossible to portray for you GE of 2001," says Jeff Immelt of General Electric.

Welch purposefully made it difficult for investors to comprehend GE's unusually smooth quarterly statistics. Immelt, too, was coming to terms with the fact that GE was in terrible trouble. He might have reined in GE Capital, sold off some of the company's riskier financial holdings, and put the money back into production. Immelt didn't want to be the one to end GE's record-breaking quarterly earnings streak. So, in a hurry, he went to GE Capital for profits and once again beat earnings.

On CNBC, Gross stated, "GE has been enveloped in mystery." However, he also made a more basic criticism that obviously questioned Welch's reliability. Gross, a pioneer of Pimco, and a significant institutional investor, was famed for his long memoranda and foresight. John Gross: GE Capital's success was built on its wheeling and dealing in the short-term paper market, as well as its never-ending acquisitions. "GE increases earnings not so much through management acumen or the diversity of their operations, as Welch and Immelt assert, but by acquiring firms," says Gross.

He claims that GE would be dangerously exposed in the case of a catastrophe. "I believe that if Jesus Christ himself had gone in after him, he would have had a difficult time," Tom Tiller says.

"I had the world by the ass"

Welch was living it up as Nardelli toiled away at Home Depot, McNerney tried to recreate 3M, and Immelt wrestled with GE. The assaults shook the global economy, but Welch was unfazed. He was preparing for a second act, cementing his status as Manager of the Century. "It seemed as if I had joined forces with the enemy," Suzy recalls of some of the actual business journalists on the crew. The Welch profile was redone by a fresh team of reporters, and it was released as "Jack on Jack."

Though Welch left GE in September 2001, the company never truly ceased working for him. Wetlaufer began her career as a local reporter and went on to write the novel Judgment Call, about a beautiful, feisty female reporter who falls in love with one of her sources, a Miami cocaine dealer. Welch would be entitled to the generosity of GE stockholders until his death, even if he quit the firm. When the details were made public, it caused a stir. Welch's penthouse at the Trump International Hotel & Tower, with its panoramic views of Central Park and the substantial costs that come with such a regal residence, was one of them.

Box tickets at the Metropolitan Opera at Lincoln Center and courtside seats at Madison Square Garden were available in Manhattan. Less than a year later, Larry Bossidy got an essentially identical provision incorporated into his Honeywell contract. Welch's retirement gift created a precedent, with other corporations offering comparable packages to their CEOs. "GREED" was the cover of the New York Daily News, which featured Welch. Welch and Wetlaufer married after Welch and Beasley split, with Beasley taking home $183 million. That didn't stop NBC, which was then under Immelt's control, from approving The Apprentice, giving Trump a new lease on fame and money.

For Welch, it was the same. His first year out of the corporate world was rocky, and the flaws in GE's foundation may have begun to emerge.

Chapter Five

Rotten Apples

"Terrible excesses"

GE wasn't the only one. The Texas energy corporation was regarded as one of the best-managed companies in the country prior to its downfall in 2001. Dennis Kozlowski was selected as one of Businessweek's "Top 25 Managers of the Year" in 2002. He was already set to make tens of millions of dollars as the CEO of a large American firm. In the middle of this rapid expansion, he turned to crime and stole $150 million from the company's coffers.

Kozlowski said he aimed to be a "combination of what Jack Welch put together at GE and Warren Buffett's very practical thoughts on how to go about producing a return for shareholders," citing Welch as an example. "It looked to the public as if all of the business was filled with nasty people—a big orchard of rotten apples," says GE co-founder Al Immelt. Immelt claims he is proud of his involvement in fostering a culture at GE where such wrongdoing was tolerated. While Welch, who had recently retired, didn't appear to recognize his own part in fostering a culture where such wrongdoing was tolerated, even he could see that something was wrong.

"The employees will still be cowering"

Even Boeing, which had been one of the paragons of American industrialism for so long, was embroiled in a scandal by the early 2000s. With a business culture centered on the bottom line, he replaced Harry Stonecipher, who was forced to quit after having an affair with a subordinate. As the Boeing board sought a new CEO, they went to Jim McNerney, one of the individuals who came close to succeeding Welch.

Despite the fact that the former light bulb executive was not an engineer, he completed his stint at GE as the head of the aircraft engines division, an experience that provided him good ties at Boeing's top levels and a working understanding of aviation market. Managers' pay would be related not merely to the company's stock price, but also to the financial performance of their own business groups under the new structure. They were calculating how much money they might save by pinching pennies along the way. Welch's joy in making his staff shiver was also shared by McNerney. McNerney's comments, according to union head Tom Buffenbarger, are a reminder that "the Jack Welch style of anti-personnel management is still alive and well at Boeing." The corporation need a new jet that could go over 7,000 miles without refueling.

When McNerney came, the 787 program was still in its infancy, but the new CEO recognized an opportunity to make his imprint.

Around 35% of parts on earlier Boeing planes were outsourced to contractors, while Boeing built the majority of the components in-house. The Boeing 787 Dreamliner was developed and manufactured in South Carolina, which has the lowest union participation in the United States. Much of the design and technical work on the new jet was done by Boeing's subcontractors. Managers in South Carolina were urged not to recruit workers who had previously participated in organized labor in order to avoid a prospective unionization effort.

Boeing received exactly what it paid for. Many staff were concerned about the Dreamliners' safety when they left the facility. "I've informed my wife that I'll never travel on it," said Joseph Clayton, a production technician.

"Winning"

Winning: The Answers: Confronting 74 of Today's Toughest Business Questions was written by them. According to Dan Rather of 60 Minutes, Welch is one of the most successful corporate CEOs in the history of American industry. Welch adds, "And he's obsessed with winning." When Dan Rather featured Welch and Wetlaufer on 60 Minutes in 2005, he said, "No question, Jack Welch, the retiring CEO of GE, is one of the most successful corporate CEOs in the history of American industry." "They're co-leaders," says the narrator.

In 2005, the magazine Newsweek, which popularized the term "Neutron Jack," had Welch on the cover with the title "How to Win." Welch made the ludicrous claim during a panel discussion with Nobel Laureate economist Joseph Stiglitz that no successful business has ever thrived with a strongly unionized workforce, ignoring the glory days of the American auto and steel industries, to name just two examples. Welch utilized the same hard-nosed techniques he used at GE to create dread in the aspiring principals.

Despite his efforts, the initiative had minimal impact on the school system in the city. "They are!" exclaims the narrator. Welch became chairman of the NYC Leadership Academy, an institution founded to advise Incoming York City public school teachers and educate new administrators, in 2003, brimming with confidence. Welch felt he could assist restore the public schools in New York City since he was an expert in the field. He believed he could accomplish it because he was a great CEO, not a reformer of education.

Clifford saw Welch's brand strength and saw an opportunity, so they met shortly after, and Clifford presented Welch with the concept of starting an online MBA program. Soon after, the two men founded the Jack Welch Management Institute, an online MBA program that included Welch and others of his loyal acolytes, like Jim McNerney, as instructors on occasion. Welch altered himself, just as he had converted GE from a sleepy industrial behemoth to a supercharged diversified multinational. He didn't give away large quantities of money or think hard about how his tenure as the CEO of a major American corporation had influenced the country's fate.

"You could feel his presence"

Following 9/11, GE made a large stake in security technology businesses, spending $1 billion on two explosive detection companies. The companies never grew significantly, and in 2009, Immelt sold his controlling stake in the companies for a large loss. Welch's warning to Langone on the eve of his retirement, that Immelt was an imprudent dealmaker, seemed prescient. Jeff Immelt, the CEO of General Electric, sold the appliance division to Haier, a Chinese corporation, for $5.4 billion. The outcome was a characteristic of globalization that Welch probably didn't see coming: American workers suddenly worked for a Chinese company and were paid less than they were when the factory was still owned by GE.

GE Capital continues to buy specialty finance companies, this time investing $4 billion in a real estate finance company. Under Welch, financial services have never contributed more than 41% of GE's profits. That percentage increased to over 60% under Immelt's leadership. "That man's influence was incredibly deep," says Aaron Dignan. "This is going to hurt before it gets better," Dignan says.

Immelt and his colleagues were also joined by Eric Ries, a consultant and author of The Lean Startup. "He had essentially the same position within GE as Thomas Edison," Ries stated. As Immelt launched Ecomagination, 30 Rock, Fey's NBC and GE parody, mocked the endeavor, with Alec Baldwin's CEO character, Jack Donaghy, inspired by Welch, advocating his own environmental cause.

Chapter Six

Bad Trades

"I almost fell out of my seat"

Subprime mortgages provided an endless supply of free money to anyone who thought they could make a profit by flipping a property while the market was still rising. In the years following 9/11, despite the risks, lenders granted millions of subprime mortgages. These dubious loans were bundled into mortgage-backed securities by Wall Street corporations. GE Capital had grown into trading, private equity, and high-interest credit cards under Welch's leadership. Nonetheless, in 2004, with GE looking for profit anywhere it could, Immelt decided to buy Western Asset Mortgage Capital, a prominent subprime lender, for $500 million.

GE had purchased a Japanese firm that funded consumer loans during Welch's tenure, and Immelt bought it. The financial market contagion had expanded well beyond the United States, and GE Capital's strategy of pursuing acquisitions all around the world appeared to be foolish. Even if the United States' capital markets collapsed, the global financial system would have enough cash to support GE Capital's frenzied deal making and lending activities. GE posted first-quarter profits in April 2008 that were considerably below Wall Street's estimates. Three days later, the investment bank Bear Stearns went bankrupt, causing the first severe financial market tremors.

Immelt, and encouraged, maintained his upbeat demeanor. "Investors now realize that GE spends the last several weeks of the quarter to 'fine-tune' it's financial service portfolios to ensure that its profits targets are met," GE analyst Heymann noted at the time. Part of what made the act so alluring was the fact that it wasn't fully evident how Welch and later Immelt made it all work. The cash was needed after the corporation reported a 22 percent decline in quarterly profits, with GE Capital reporting a 38 percent drop. Immelt was compensated $25 million for his resolution to do rid of GE Capital once and for all.

"Get a gun out and shoot him"

Under Immelt, GE's market value had plummeted by hundreds of billions of dollars, and the news only got worse. Welch, on the other hand, was enraged in private. Jeff Immelt, CEO of General Electric: Not only could anybody have controlled GE in the 1990s, but so could a German shepherd. The SEC resolved broad accounting fraud accusations against GE in 2009. In order to boost its stock price, the corporation inflated earnings.

Welch had left him "a sack of crap," as Immelt put it. From 1995 through 2004, the SEC discovered that GE met or exceeded analyst estimates in every quarter. At GE, manipulating profits had obviously become an art form. The SEC's head of Enforcement stated, "GE twisted the accounting standards past the breaking point." To resolve the dispute, GE agreed to pay the government $50 million in a settlement. The agreement allowed GE to pretend that the misbehavior was an honest error perpetrated by a few bad apples.

The implication was unmistakable: similar techniques were being used during the height of Welch's influence. Even while neither Welch nor Immelt was to blame for the catastrophe, GE was profoundly entwined with a poisonous financial system when the dominoes began to fall. GE Capital became the polar opposite of what it was intended to be, tearing down rather than building up the middle class. The embracing of financial complexity was a natural outgrowth of GE Capital's black box ethos. Even though GE had no participation in the crisis, the basic dynamics that led to so much risk being accumulated by so few mirrored the Welchian viewpoint. And the perpetrators of the crisis—bankers, financiers, and executives who saddled homeowners with unsustainable debt, raised interest rates, and packaged bad mortgages into products so toxic that they poisoned the entire economy—went unpunished, enjoying the same impunity that white-collar criminals enjoy.

"The dumbest idea in the world"

Following the financial crisis, a new generation of activists took to the streets to protest widening inequality and the policies that cause it. Outrage erupted on the streets as the actual extent of those responsible for the disaster became clear. The Occupy Wall Street movement began in New York and quickly expanded to Oakland, London, and dozens of other cities across the globe. As audiences throughout the world gathered on the streets to protest the repercussions of Welchism, what began as drum circles grew into a global series of rallies, several of which prompted deadly police repression.

"Shareholder value is the stupidest notion in the world," GE CEO Jack Welch stated after the financial crisis. Welch called shareholder value "the stupidest notion in the world," but he didn't say it was wrong. For Welch's critique of shareholder value, Forbes published headlines like "The Dumbest Idea in the World: Maximizing Shareholder Value." Welch was on a massive push to erase his career's flaws and maintain the idea that he was the Manager of the Century.

"The Dumbest Idea in the World: Maximizing Shareholder Value," according to Forbes, and Welch is sometimes credited with "seeing the light" and becoming "one of the sharpest opponents of shareholder value."

"Go, go, go"

American Airlines was ready to place a large order with Airbus for a fleet of new A320neos, Airbus' single-aisle competitor to Boeing's 737. Boeing made a choice in a couple of days: it would remodel the 737 once more, but this time it would be faster and less expensive than developing a whole new jet. Gerard Arpey, the CEO of American Airlines, one of Boeing's finest clients, was on the line. Dennis Muilenburg, a Boeing veteran who rose through the ranks in the company's military division, took over as CEO. One of the dark horses in the race to succeed Welch, Dave Calhoun, was appointed to the board.

Choosing an engineer from inside Boeing's ranks signaled that the GE culture, which had lasted over two decades, was beginning to erode. The plane's tagline was "Max Efficiency, Max Reliability," and airlines all over the world rapidly placed orders for thousands of the new planes, making it Boeing's best-selling airliner ever. The technology is based on a weak bit of metal that gauges the plane's pitch, according to engineers. The final version of MCAS that was introduced to the Max was never completely examined by the FAA. A description of MCAS was included in the pilot's manual for a long time.

Because MCAS was a new function on the Max, Boeing considered emphasizing it and making it an important part of pilots' understanding of the upgraded jet. The 737 Max was designed to be as comparable to the previous version of the jet, the 737NG, as feasible. Pilots that flew the NG would be able to manage the Max without undergoing considerable extra training, according to Boeing. Southwest Airlines was assured by Boeing that if pilots needed simulator training, the cost of each Max would be reduced by $1 million. One note from a test pilot said, "This airplane is created by clowns, who are then monitored by monkeys."

"For the first time in my life, I'm afraid to put my family on a Boeing jet," says GE employee Ed Pierson. It was the same kind of pressure that Welch had applied within GE's facilities, but this time, lives were at stake.

"Unbelievable jobs numbers"

He once sketched an image of a human hand with its middle finger up on NBC's Decision Desk during a news program regarding George Stephanopoulos. "That liberal jerk!" While homeowners and employees were forgotten in the government's reaction, the stock market was back on track within a few years after the crisis, and even corporations like GE and Boeing were thriving again. However, in retirement, Welch went from being just political to becoming outright conspiratorial. The irony was as rich as Welch himself because GE was at its peak during Clinton's presidency.

"In regards to today's jobs data, I agree with former GE CEO Jack Welch," Republican congressman Allen West tweeted.

Even then-reality television star Donald Trump joined the chorus of conspiracy theorists, declaring Welch's false claim "100 percent true" and accusing the Obama administration of "monkeying about" with the data. Welch was at the forefront of a misinformation campaign, but he wasn't alone. But their lies found an eager audience, propelling Trump to the White House and setting the basis for Pizzagate, QAnon, and the never-ending stream of lies to come from President Trump himself.

"The wealthiest persons made the most errors"

Welch and Immelt exemplified America's shift away from manufacturing and toward financialization. The General Electric Company and a large portion of the larger economy may have been wiped out if GE Capital had failed. "We deemphasized technology when some of America's rivals were ramping up on manufacturing and R&D," he told an audience at West Point in late 2009. Alstom, a French business that makes power turbines, was purchased by GE for $10.6 billion, making it the corporation's biggest sale ever. However, as the contract was finalized, the cost of solar panels and wind turbines fell, making renewable energy more cost-competitive.

GE was a shell of the corporation Welch had built more than a decade after Immelt took control. Sanders continued, launching an attack against Welchism as a whole. In a Washington Post op-ed, Immelt retorted, claiming that GE was a force for good. And General Electric is doing an excellent job of evading taxes. Sanders stated, "General Electric was founded in this nation by American workers and American consumers."

In 2015, the year he secured the catastrophic Alstom contract and GE's corporate aircraft became a symbol of all that was wrong with the corporation, he earned $33 million. By 2017, the board of directors had had enough, and Immelt was fired. "These two former GE CEOs have a lot of bad blood," a source said. "Given the decisions Immelt took, Welch has misgivings about Immelt, and Immelt has been dissatisfied by some aspects of the Welch legacy." In thinking about the guy who plucked him for the most coveted job in corporate America, Immelt was similarly terse. On June 19, 2018, GE was removed from the Dow Jones Industrial Average, the bluest of blue-chip indices and a barometer for the American economy, as a result of Welch's disastrous actions.

Though GE had claimed to be out of the insurance sector throughout Immelt's tenure as CEO, this was not the case. Walgreens Boots Alliance, a pharmacy business, would take the role of GE. However, seeing General Electric in such a sad shape served as a stark reminder of the company's illustrious past and present. "GE no longer qualifies as one of our country's most significant corporations," one money manager said. The corporation, which had long stopped coming to the rescue with last-minute earnings, was caught up in Welchism. After all, America wasn't so much a country that manufactured appliances and jet engines as it was a country that consumed prescription medications and processed meals.

Chapter Seven

Negative Externalities

"We're not treated as human beings"

The positive influence of GE on the globe was measured by all of the excellent things it brought to life, but under Welch, the negatives began to pile up. Corporations cause as much harm as they do well, from catastrophic climate change to hollowed-out towns abandoned by industries seeking cheap labor overseas. The Economics of Welfare further elaborated on the notion of "externalities" in business, which refers to the unintended consequences of economic activity. Pigou could not have envisaged the tremendous range, magnitude, and severity of the damages that would arise from the corporate sector today on his lush Cambridge campus a century ago. The three fundamental characteristics of Welchism are still prevalent in the current economy: downsizing, dealmaking, and financialization.

Consider shrinking. Companies are attempting to redefine what it means to have a job in the aftermath of the gig economy. Depending on the industry, the new reduction takes numerous shapes. What started with Jack Welch's explorations into outsourcing—shifting people off GE's payroll and onto service providers—has now been carried to a new extreme, with firms relying on contractors, freelancers, and the gig economy for as much labor as possible. Stack ranking became popular in the years after Welch introduced it at GE, not just at Ford and 3M, where it led to lawsuits, but also in the computer industry.

Adam Neumann, the creator of WeWork, has a goal of laying off 20% of the company's employees per year. Amazon's human resource policies are meant to ensure that the great majority of workers have only the most tenuous ties to the corporation. Amazon CEO Jeff Bezos, like Welch before him, seemed to arrive on the job with a zealot's belief that employees were inherently replaceable. Bezos reasoned that if his staff wasn't threatened with dismissal, they wouldn't work as hard. "Our tendency as humans is to use as little energy as possible to obtain what we want or need," the executive remarked. Employees at Amazon are increasingly controlled by software rather than by human people.

Amazon's revenues show the financial benefits of letting machines look after people. However, having an algorithm as a boss might be troublesome for the workforce. Some employees have started to remind management that they are not simply a part of the data stream. Amazon, like GE under Welch, appears to be built to chew up and spit out employees. After three years, Bezos stopped giving mandated raises and began looking for methods to fire employees who were not adequately engaged.

Amazon is so devoted to the concept of permanent transient labor that it pays hourly employees cash bonuses if they leave. Amazon, like GE, has a rating system for its employees. Jeff Bezos, the CEO of Amazon, may be compared to Jack Welch of his day. In 2015, the New York Times released a report on Amazon's poor labor conditions.

"We've sort of put it all together"

Comcast had purchased NBC Universal from GE, thirty years after Welch had bought the company as part of the RCA merger. The firm would be sold for a huge loss to private investors before being integrated with Discovery Communications. The AT&T-Discovery transaction was more than just a power play by a Welch protégé. As a result, the number of publicly traded firms in the United States is now around half of what it was during Welch's heyday. Three-quarters of all industries in the United States are much more consolidated than they were twenty-five years ago.

Corporate consolidation has lowered average American earnings by $10,000 per year, according to some estimates. Welch's downsizing, dealmaking, and financialization have all been incorporated into AT&T's corporate structure. A group of Brazilian investors created 3G Capital, a private equity firm that owns brands such as Budweiser, Burger King, and Kraft Heinz. Ambev, Brazil's largest beer manufacturer, purchased Anheuser-Busch in

1999, making it the world's largest brewer. When it comes to lowering expenses and boosting prices on customers, AB InBev became known for doing it in an unemotional manner.

All the while, 3G discovered methods to breathe fresh life into Welch's strategies. "The yearly reports from GE were like the Bible to us." Buffett, like Welch, is equally astute, and he requires the same unwavering emphasis on profitability that Welch did at GE. Employees were only allowed one personal item per workstation and were required to work Saturdays. Heinz was already on a tight budget, and cutting back on printer paper would only get him so far. The united firm, Kraft Heinz, quickly became one of the world's largest food corporations.

Buffett will be worth $26 billion in 2021 thanks to well-timed stock transactions and ownership positions. In total, more than a quarter of Pittsburgh's workforce was laid off. Welchism's defining tactics—downsizing, dealmaking, and financialization—were still being used at one of the world's largest corporations two decades into the twenty-first century. The negative externalities are innumerable, and they can be seen in the corporations themselves, in the employees who suffer, and in data that reveals that this land's wealth is not equally divided, not even close. The Jack Welch manner of doing business—and occasionally Welch's personal tutelage—has left a path of disaster at company after company.

The only exceptions are Amazon, 3G, AT&T, and Under Armour. Approximately 44% of working Americans earn less than $18,000 per year on average. Places like Erie and Schenectady, where GE formerly employed tens of thousands of people, are struggling, while Denver and Boston are booming. Also, rather than the Rust Belt cities and rural areas that prospered during the Golden Age, wealth is being concentrated geographically, with superstar businesses centered in metropolitan centers. A top executive of a big American corporation today earns in a year what an average employee of that corporation would earn in 320 years.

Welch: The compensation ratio between CEOs and employees stayed steady for nearly three decades following WWII. With a median net worth of well over $10 million, the richest 1% of Americans now own about 45 percent of the country's wealth. Then, about the time Welch became CEO of GE, the trend lines started to diverge. According to Welch, by 2020, Jeff Bezos, Bill Gates, and Mark Zuckerberg would hold as much money as the poorest half of the US economy combined. John D. Rockefeller, Henry Clay Frick, Andrew Carnegie, and George Fisher Baker accounted for 0.85% of American wealth in 1913.

In 1913, the richest 0.01 percent of Americans owned 2% of the country's wealth; now, they own 10%. Welch: Four decades of Welchism have inevitably resulted in such stark numbers. Amazon employees are watched by robots, and Jeff Bezos can now afford to send himself to space. Corporations' tax payments have decreased, but buybacks and dividends have increased. Welchism has emptied manufacturing communities while lining the pockets of Wall Street. This is the world that Welch has left us.

Two Crashes

With 189 passengers on board, Lion Air Flight 610 took off from Jakarta on October 29, 2018. The jet was a brand-new Boeing 737 Max, one of the hundreds that Lion Air had acquired. MCAS, the new technology installed on the Max, was found to have had a part in the disaster within days, according to the retrieved flight recorder data. However, there remained a baffling unwillingness at Boeing's top echelons to realize the gravity of the problem the business was now facing. The nose of the Max would suddenly sink without notice.

Boeing hinted as much in public remarks, while senior Boeing executives reaffirmed Max's safety in private conversations with American Airlines pilots. Boeing would have faced a full-fledged problem if it had fully comprehended what occurred off the coast of Jakarta. Boeing stated that it planned to replace the MCAS software, implying that the plane was defective. Boeing CEO Dennis Muilenburg said that the business will increase its dividend by 20% and spend $20 billion on stock buybacks. A Boeing 737 Max took off from Addis Ababa, Ethiopia, on March 10, 2019, bound for Nairobi, Kenya.

The jet crashed into a desolate field six minutes after takeoff, killing all 157 persons on board. Almost every country's regulators had grounded the Max within days. President Trump was phoned by GE CEO Bill Muilenburg, who assured him that the Max was secure. The FAA was hesitant to halt Boeing's most significant airliner, so the Max continued to fly in the United States for several more days. Dennis Muilenburg, the CEO of GE, came across as robotic and lacked the necessary capabilities to deal with a problem of this size.

It appears that Boeing was aware of the MCAS risk and allowed the Max to continue flying. Boeing had cut manufacturing of the Max by half by July, indicating that the grounding would be lengthy and costly. "The second disaster constituted corporate manslaughter," one of the Ethiopian crash victims' families alleged. As Boeing tinkered with MCAS, other issues with the Max surfaced. Dave Calhoun was a long shot to succeed Welch as chairman of the Boeing board of directors.

As a result of the Max accidents, the first top executive to be sacked was Kevin McAllister. They promoted Dave Calhoun, a former GE executive who was a dark horse candidate to succeed Welch, as chairman in his place. Boeing was once again led by a Welch follower. Natalie Kitroeff and I were never permitted an interview with the new CEO during that period. Along with my colleague Natalie Kitroeff, I was one of the primary reporters on the Boeing story over the following year.

The Boeing Leadership Center was created around a château that GE's John Stonecipher purchased while leading McDonnell Douglas and transformed into Boeing's own Crotonville. Calhoun was now utilizing the center as a temporary office while he attempted to resurrect the firm, trying to harness his GE origins. Welch had died the day before, on March 1, 2020, at the age of eighty-four. Natalie and I grilled Calhoun for almost an hour on his role as CEO of Boeing, his choice to stick with Muilenburg for so long, and what he may do to turn the firm around. "If anyone had run over the rainbow for the pot of gold on stock, it would have been him," Calhoun said. "It also demonstrates our leadership's flaws." Boeing CEO John Calhoun was belligerent and accusatory, displaying the same bravado as Jack Welch.

Calhoun apologized to the company's top executives in a letter. Even the relatives of those who died in the crash couldn't overlook the resemblance. The loss of Calhoun's "lifetime mentor," Welch, shocked and distracted him, he added. Calhoun worked under Jack Welch at General Electric, according to Samya Stumo. Welchism had infected America's most powerful aerospace firm, killing 346 people.

Nadia and Michael became de facto organizers for the victims' families after the second tragedy. Boeing has been hurtling toward a moment like this since it turned its back on engineering in favor of short-term profitability.

"A Donald Trump, a Jack Welch"

Jack Welch worked on real estate ventures with Donald Trump, earning him legitimacy and endorsing his candidacy. The Apprentice on NBC offered Trump a national platform and a new wealth in 2004. For Trump, Welch was the epitome of the CEO power that Neutron Jack previously possessed. Jack Welch's admiration for Donald Trump grew into something bigger than he could have dreamed. Welch gave the real estate swindler a patina of credibility by spending so much time with him.

"Whenever he turns up, it's practically must-see TV," Welch added. Donald Trump raged against the world that Welch helped build during his campaign. The entirety of Trump's campaign appeared to be a reaction against Welchism. While he blamed "Washington" in general and Democrats in particular, he also blamed CEOs like Welch. The huckster of the Millenium had duped the Manager of the Century.

Men like Welch, Immelt, Nardelli, and McNerney redirected the flow of income from Schenectady employees to their own bank accounts. "I give him an A on the business community's morale," Welch says. The group was never used for anything useful. There was no obvious plan or policy emanating from this gathering of corporate intellectuals. Merck Pharma's Ken Frazier resigned from President Donald Trump's manufacturing committee.

With the exception of a handful who wished to support the president, the choice was practically unanimous. Standing behind Trump after his words in the aftermath of Charlottesville required a special type of devotion. When asked why they elected to join Donald Trump's business advisory groups, Jack Welch and Jack McNerney gave their reasons. For the vast majority of mainstream CEOs, the answer was self-evident. But for them, the equation was a little more complicated: Trump was one of their own. Neutron Jack's values have now pervaded all aspects of American society.

Chapter Eight

Beyond Welchism

"A more responsible business model"

Unilever, the Anglo-Dutch consumer products business, was taken over by Paul Polman in 2009. Prior to entering the corporate world, Polman trained to become a Jesuit priest. In the commercial sector, he applied some of the empathy he had developed in the church. In the United Kingdom, he battled for six-day work weeks and pensions. In Port Sunlight, there was no smoking and no drinking, which improved life expectancy.

He wanted to convey a message to the firm that he was serious about making it more sustainable. Within four months, the company's stock began to increase once more. Unilever received an unsolicited purchase bid from Kraft Heinz. The Welch imitators at 3G Capital ran Kraft Heinz. The perspectives of Polman and the Brazilians on how to operate a firm were starkly different.

On paper, everything seemed good, but it was essentially two opposing economic systems. When he took over Unilever, he was an aberration, one of the few CEOs ready to challenge the existing quo. Today's CEOs have devised strategies to combat Welchism. The CEO of Paypal was taken aback when he discovered that many of his lowest-paid employees are struggling to make ends meet. The corporation established a $5 million fund to assist employees who were facing financial difficulties.

The fund was inundated with applications as soon as it was announced. Joel Schulman, a co-founder of PayPal, was taken aback by how many of his workers were struggling to make ends meet. Between paychecks, two-thirds of respondents claimed they were short on funds. PayPal's lower-paid employees have access to a four-part financial wellness program. Paypal's CEO, Bruce Schulman, slashed staff healthcare expenditures by 60%.

He also provided every employee the opportunity to acquire business equity. The shares of PayPal more than quadrupled in the year after the program's launch. It cost tens of millions of dollars but had a huge influence on the lives of workers. PayPal CEO Dan Schulman and co-founder Jason Polman are redefining the norms that have previously guided CEOs in their business decisions. They are trying to invest in their personnel rather than layoffs as a knee-jerk reaction to misfortune. It's the polar opposite of Welchism.

"Where the fiduciary duty is starting to move"

Stakeholder capitalism is a throwback to capitalism's Golden Age, a return to the collectivist ethos that predated Welch's arrival. For decades, Klaus Schwab, a German scholar, and creator of the World Economic Forum has advocated for this method. The B Corporation movement established a framework for assessing a company's entire impact on employees, the environment, and society. Some larger corporations, such as Danone, a French dairy company, have earned the B Corp certification. Patagonia, Seventh Generation, and other brands joined, and even larger firms like Danone, a French dairy company, and Natura, a major Brazilian cosmetics company, received the B Corp mark of approval.

According to Larry Fink, CEO of BlackRock, "too many firms are shying away from investing in their future growth." In an open letter to corporate America that year, Fink stated, "It concerns us that, in the aftermath of the financial crisis, many firms have shied away from investing in their future growth." After decades of sticking to Welch's principles, even the Business Roundtable changed its mind. "We pledge to provide value to all of them in order to ensure the long-term prosperity of our businesses, communities, and country."

Offer Better Pay and Benefits

Workers should be paid a livable wage as a matter of course. According to studies, rising worker pay does not result in increased unemployment or inflation. Companies should devote a larger portion of their revenues to finance the benefits of their lowest-paid employees.

Share Profits, and Equity

Companies should make it a practice to share gains with their employees. This can take the shape of simple profit-sharing schemes in some cases. According to research, these initiatives promote employee morale and productivity, resulting in stronger businesses. In today's economy, real wealth is produced through investing rather than working.

Upskill Workers

Amazon and other large corporations might benefit from establishing new career paths for their employees. Companies should also play a bigger role in ensuring that their employees are well-prepared. Workers who have upskilled are better prepared if they quit their job or if layoffs are necessary.

Put Workers on Boards

In the 1970s, Chrysler appointed the president of its largest union, the United Auto Workers, to its board of directors. In Europe, co-determination, often known as "co-determination," is prospering. Workers in Germany, for example, have the right to elect half of the supervisory boards.

Think Long Term

CEOs, according to Welch, should reject the market's tyranny and embrace a more patient approach to growth. Mergers and acquisitions should also be approached with greater caution.

Magnificent CEOs can only bring us so far; legislators must take decisive measures to establish an economy that is really egalitarian.

Raise the Minimum Wage

The federal government needs to intervene and increase the minimum wage. It's long overdue and would have a huge impact on millions of people's lives right now. If the minimum wage had kept pace with inflation over the last half-century, it would be more than three times its present level.

Raise Taxes

After decades of conservative economic policies that have whittled down the revenue base, tax reform is an essential adjustment. A wealth tax on the richest 1% of the population might raise $3.7 trillion over ten years. Tax benefits should no longer be used to entice businesses to invest in their localities. Regulators are likely to take a wide view of whether transactions are worth their time. Executive pay limitations would eliminate some of the most severe causes of income disparity. These policies are not only moral and right, but they are also profitable.

"Jack paved the way"

Many people adored Jack Welch, and he had a large circle of friends and acquaintances. Suzy, his widow, delivered poignant mourning for her husband, emphasizing his enormous clout. The Covid-19 epidemic was sweeping the United States at the time of Jack Welch's burial. Greene, Bob: The epidemic served as a litmus test for businesses who talked about shareholder value. Greene: Within weeks after Covid's implementation, most companies would continue to prioritize shareholders and executives.

During the epidemic, Amazon employed around 100,000 people. Jeff Bezos, the company's founder, became the first person to be worth $200 billion. Office workers were laid off by Microsoft, Oracle, Comcast, and AT&T in 2020. Amazon's starting hourly wage for entry-level employees was $15. The CEO of Norwegian Cruise Line received $36.4 million in 2020, despite the fact that his firm lost $4 billion due to the epidemic.

The study discovered an inverse relationship between virtue signaling and actual virtuous behavior. Senator deems the statement of the Business Roundtable "an empty Publicity Stunt." In Larry Culp's first full year as CEO, GE's stock dropped another 8%. One of the company's remaining profitable businesses, jet engines, vanished from the market. The Securities and Exchange Commission penalized GE $200 million for deceiving investors about the source of earnings in its power division.

The corporation made no admissions or denials of guilt, just declaring that "no changes or revisions to our financial accounts are necessary." GE has officially confirmed that it would disband once and for all. Jeff Immelt: I didn't have any basis for that. Getting up and saying, 'Hey, this place is messed up.' Immelt expressed sorrow for not acting more quickly after 9/11. He extolled his achievements and scoffed at suggestions that he had overpaid for transactions.

The split between the Golden Age of Capitalism and the period of shareholder capitalism was formed by Jack Welch. Welch was the first CEO to take a profitable business and turn it around. He was also the first to employ dealmaking to broaden the company's reach into any industry. Many of our largest corporations continue to focus on short-term gains, undervalue workers, falsify figures, and lavish unjustified bonuses on CEOs. The negative externalities of Welch's business model have become too obvious to ignore.

More than good-hearted CEOs and altruistic officials will be required to bring Welchism to a close. There is no legislation requiring businesses to increase shareholder value. We'll have to come up with a new set of common objectives that encourage broad economic prosperity rather than widespread inequality.

Made in the USA
Monee, IL
11 October 2022

15690518R00046